THE
TOP **10** DISTINCTIONS
BETWEEN
Dream Fulfillers
AND
Dream Killers

THE
TOP **10** DISTINCTIONS
BETWEEN
Dream Fulfillers
AND
Dream Killers

KEITH CAMERON SMITH

WKU Publishing

Published in the United States by WKU Publishing
www.keithcameronsmith.com

ISBN 978-0-9755070-5-6

First Edition

Book design by www.tothepointsolutions.com

CONTENTS

THE
TOP **10** DISTINCTIONS
BETWEEN

Dream Fulfillers
AND
Dream Killers

DISTINCTION TEN

Dream fulfillers are finishers.

Dream killers are starters.

What is your dream? Do you take time to think about your dream every day? Few people do. One of the biggest reasons for this is distractions. Sadly, many people have either not started to pursue their dreams or are sidetracked by distractions when in pursuit of their dreams.

Distractions are inevitable; they are a part of pursuing your dreams. Everyone has distractions in their lives; learning to deal with them and staying focused is a secret to seeing your dream fulfilled.

Dream fulfillers are finishers because they have learned how to deal with distractions. Dream killers start toward their dreams but they allow distractions to stop them from taking consistent action. Consistency is a key to victory. If you only pursue your dream occasionally you will eventually quit pursuing it.

How can you deal with distractions? What I

am about to tell you may sound too simple but if you haven't discovered this yet it will transform your life and help you get back on track with your dream. One of the best ways to deal with distractions is learning to say no. A distraction is something that is not in alignment with your dream. By saying no you can stay focused on your dream. Saying no to distractions is an absolute must if you are going to see your dream fulfilled. Learning to say no will strengthen your focus and increase your clarity. Always remember: clarity is power. It is powerful to finish what you start. If you allow distractions to steal your focus, then you will kill your dream.

Focus is the opposite of distraction. Staying focused simply means to consistently say yes to the things that are in alignment with your dream and no to the things that are not. Dream fulfillers are finishers because they stay focused.

What do you do when you have a distraction that you can't say no to or when there is something you can't ignore? The answer is to handle it as quickly as possible. Do not let distractions build up on you—because if you do, you will kill your dream.

Procrastination is a terrible enemy of dream fulfillers but it is a friend of dream killers. Allowing distractions to stack up can lead to overwhelm which leads to shutdown. Say no when you should and immediately take care of the things that must be done. These two simple rules will help you become a dream fulfiller.

Learn to handle distractions because they lead to disappointment.

You must learn to handle distractions because they lead to disappointment. Hear me clearly: allowing distractions to build up will lead to disappointment. When you find yourself disappointed, immediately reappoint yourself to your dream before you get discouraged.

It's okay to be disappointed, but it's not okay to be discouraged. If you have allowed yourself to become discouraged, then it is time to encourage yourself. It is your responsibility to encourage yourself. It is nice when others encourage you but if you sit around waiting for someone else to encourage you, you will spend a lot of time stuck in a rut. If you spend too much time stuck in a rut, you will end up in depression.

Did you notice all of these words start with the letter D? Distractions lead to disappointments, disappointments lead to discouragement, and discouragement leads to depression. Most people are totally unaware that they ended up in depression because they never learned how to handle distractions. Don't let distractions and your disappointments get you off track. Be a finisher.

- Say no to everything that is not in alignment with your dream.

- Things that you can't say no to must be handled as quickly as possible.

- Do not let distractions build up or you will become discouraged.

- If you do become discouraged, find a way to encourage yourself.

- If you have allowed yourself to be discouraged for so long that you are now battling with depression, then get focused on your dream again and restart taking action.

Dream fulfillers have to restart themselves toward their dream hundreds and even thousands of times before they finish what they started. Every distraction, every disappointment, every discouragement, every battle with depression is just a temporary stop for dream fulfillers. They get started again as soon as possible. Dream killers start and stop and don't get restarted. Dream fulfillers start, stop, and start again many, many times. Restarting is the difference between a goal setter and a goal achiever. A lot of people have set goals and never achieve them simply because of one of those negative D-words.

I am now going to share a positive D-word with you that makes all the difference: diligence. Diligence is the ability to start, stop, and start again. Diligence is the ability to stay focused and take consistent action. Diligence is the commitment to your dream that will cause you to work hard and carry you through to comple-

> Diligence is the ability to stay focused and take consistent action.

tion. Diligence is one of the primary characteristics of all dream fulfillers. It is a must-have to being a finisher. Diligence is a decision to work hard and do whatever it takes to achieve your dream. It is a commitment to make your dream come true in spite of the inevitable distractions and disappointments. Diligence empowers dream fulfillers to persevere. Diligence and perseverance empower you to be a finisher.

Perseverance is the power to endure tough times. Perseverance is fueled by a belief that your dream is possible and it is worth all the stuff you must go through to get it. Without perseverance, without the belief that your dream is possible and it's worth everything you are going through, you will become a dream killer. You must dream it and believe it to achieve it.

> Perseverance is the power to endure tough times.

Dream fulfillers are believers. Dream killers are doubters. Believing enables you to finish. Doubting causes you to stop after you started and not get restarted. Believe in your dream and you will develop diligence and perseverance and will overcome all the distractions, disappointments, discouragements, and depressions. Don't be a starter who becomes quitter. Be a finisher.

Dream fulfillers are finishers.

Dream killers are starters.

DISTINCTION NINE

Dream fulfillers are fully engaged.

Dream killers are only enrolled.

Being fully engaged means you consistently work hard toward your dream. Working hard toward your dream is not the same as hard work. Hard work without a dream attached is exhausting. Working hard toward your dream may be exhausting but it is also energizing. It is one of those weird paradoxes. The fatigue that comes from working hard toward your dream is accompanied by a true sense of fulfillment and that fulfillment energizes you to keep on keeping on.

People who are only enrolled may work hard, although it is usually in the wrong direction. Working hard in a direction that does not move you closer to your dream is truly hard work.

Working hard includes more than physical labor. For example, staying focused on your dream is harder for most people than digging ditches or making cold calls all day. Focus requires some serious energy. Dream fulfillers work hard to stay focused.

Dream fulfillers also work hard on inspiring and encouraging them-selves and others. I once asked a pastor of a large church what his biggest challenge was and he quickly replied, "Keeping people inspired and encouraged." Think about it. Just keeping your-self inspired and encouraged is hard work, let alone inspiring and encouraging others.

> Hard work without a dream attached is exhausting.

The reason dream fulfillers can remained fully engaged and work hard is because they believe their dreams are possible and that they are worthy of their time and efforts. Do you believe your dream is possible and worthy of your efforts? When you are certain that your dream is possible and worthy of your life you will become fully engaged in the process of making it come true. After you learn to keep yourself inspired and encouraged then you will be able to persuade others to support your dream and to take action on their dreams. When you believe in your dream, your faith becomes contagious and helps others to believe in their dreams.

> When you believe in your dream, your faith becomes contagious.

Being fully persuaded and engaged is the critical step to being able to persuade others. Persuasion is not the same as manipulation. Persuasion is positive; manipulation is negative. Persuasion puts people first. Manipulation uses people to fulfill selfish desires. Persuasion is the ability to get others to believe and therefore act in ways that benefit you and them.

Many people have been deceived and

manipulated to do things that are destructive to them. (I address deception and destruction in

> It is much easier to persevere when you are doing what you want to be doing.

greater detail in Distinction 1.) Manipulation builds a fire beneath people; persuasion builds a fire within them. Being able to persuade others is the ability to inspire them to believe in and act on their dreams.

Have To Versus Want To

When you are persuaded you work on things that you want to. Persuasion is related to perseverance. It is much easier to persevere when you are doing what you want to be doing. It is difficult to remain committed to something that you don't really want to be doing. When someone is being manipulated they are usually doing something that they feel they have to do, not what they want to do. Persuasion works with the deep desires of your heart. Manipulation works on the fears of your mind and the greed of your ego. Persuading people enlightens them to see that they want to; manip-ulating people forces them to feel as though they have to. Want to versus have to is a significant distinction between being fully engaged and being only enrolled.

> Manipulation works on the fears of your mind and the greed of your ego.

Teenagers who want to go to college do much better than those who feel they have to go to college. Adults who want to do a certain job or pursue a specific career do much better than adults who feel like they have to stay at a specific job or remain in a particular career. Are you fully engaged in your life or only enrolled?

Are you investing time, energy, and money

in things that you want to do or are you wasting them on things that you don't want to do? The choice is yours. Even if you currently do things that you believe you have

You can turn your life around and become a dream fulfiller.

to do, you can take steps toward those things that you want to do. It may take days, weeks, or years but you can turn your life around and become a dream fulfiller.

Start taking consistent action on the things that you want to be doing. Work hard to keep yourself inspired and encouraged. Make sure you are fully persuaded and that others are not manipulating you for their own selfish desires —and, of course, make sure you are not manipulating others. Being a persuader is much better than being a manipulator.

As you grow in confidence and become fully engaged in your own life, then you have a responsibility to also work hard to inspire and encourage others to pursue their dreams. Stay focused, and work hard to keep yourself inspired and encouraged and to persuade others to believe in their own dreams.

Dream fulfillers are fully engaged.

Dream killers are only enrolled.

DISTINCTION EIGHT

Dream fulfillers feed their faith and
starve their fears.

Dream killers feed their fears and
starve their faith.

Faith requires you to take action; fear causes you to take no action. Fear causes you to sit on your butt. Feed your fears too much and you will sit on your butt too much and it will get bigger and bigger and your use of the word *but* will become more frequent. I would do that BUT, I could do that BUT, I should do that BUT. I woulda, I shoulda, I coulda BUT I didn't because I let fear stop me.

Faith nourishes hope. Doubt nourishes fear. Living in fear does not necessarily mean there is something horrifying or terrifying that is scaring you. It could mean that you are living in doubt. Doubt is the door that fear enters through. Doubt is the spoon that feeds your fears. Remember the often-quoted, seldom-understood Scripture: Faith is the substance of things hoped for.

> Doubt is the spoon that feeds your fears.

28

Faith starts with the simple belief "I can." As you feed your faith, it will grow to the level of "I will." As you continue to feed your faith, it will grow to the level of "I am" and as you continue to feed your faith, it will grow to the substance of "I did." I call this the four levels of faith: I can, I will, I am, I did.

> The four levels of faith: I can, I will, I am, I did.

When your faith is young you feed it by your thoughts; as it grows a bit, you feed it by your thoughts and your words. As the Scriptures say, the power of life and death are in your tongue and YOU shall declare a thing and it shall come to pass and you shall have whatsoever you saith. As you feed your faith with your thoughts and words it will grow to the place of faith that Jesus spoke about, which is the level of action. My savior, my Lord, my friend said, "My meat is to do the will of Him who sent me." You feed your faith by taking action. You feed your faith by doing what you are supposed to be doing with your life. You prove your faith by the things you do.

Can you accomplish your dream? Feed your faith by your thoughts, words, and actions and you can and you will. Feed your fears and you won't. How do you kill fear? By starving it to death. You starve your fears by refusing to think, speak, or act in alignment with them. If you are afraid, you can't accomplish your dream; so simply acknowledge the fear and tell it you are not going to feed it anymore. You are going to choose to believe you can.

> Feed your faith by doing what you are supposed to be doing with your life.

Faith and fear are choices and most people are in a pattern of feeding one or the other.

Whatever you feed grows and gets stronger. Whatever you starve gets weaker and dies. Feed your faith and starve your fears.

What are you consciously choosing to put into your mind and allowing to exit your mouth? Are you choosing to put things in your mind that pertain to your dream or are you letting others feed your mind?

Feed your faith by thinking, talking about, and taking action toward your dream.

The more responsibility you take for the thoughts you think and the words you speak the more you will feed your faith with the meat of taking action. The less responsibility you take for the thoughts you think and the words you speak the more others will feed your fears and cause you to sit on your butt.

Feed your faith by thinking, talking about, and taking action toward your dream. Starve your fears by not thinking and talking about them.

Dream fulfillers feed their faith and starve their fears.

Dream killers feed their fears and starve their faith.

DISTINCTION SEVEN

Dream fulfillers build a life.

Dream killers make a living.

Building a life and fulfilling your dream requires a balance of faith, family, friends, fitness, and finances. If you work on just one of these areas and neglect the others you will not be able to build a life or fulfill your dream. But, if you focus on balancing these five areas you will build a life that is meaningful and rewarding. These five areas make up your life and each one of them influences the others.

I have never met anyone who has all five of these areas in balance all of the time. Life is dynamic, not static. Building a life is a constant balancing act. While you are pursuing your dream you will find that there are stages and seasons when you will be more engaged in one area of your life than others. Just because you are more engaged in one part of your life than another during a certain season doesn't mean that you are neglecting the other areas. Just be sure that you remain aware of each area and spend time nurturing each one on a consistent basis. The more you nurture each area the more mature you become. Being mature is not a level anyone arrives at, it is an ongoing process. As people

Life is dynamic, not static. Building a life is a constant balancing act.

mature they are better able to enjoy the season they are in while looking forward to the coming season with peace instead of stress.

Spring, Summer, Fall, Winter

Having an understanding of the natural seasons gives you valuable insight for the seasons of life. Without this understanding you can waste a lot of time living in the past or worrying about the future—when you should be focused on the here and now.

In the maturing process there are different

seasons in each area of your life. In the physical world, spring is the time to prepare the ground and plant seeds. Summer is the time to be fighting the weeds, fertilizing the soil, and making sure your crop is getting enough water. Fall is for harvesting. It is a time of intense work and it is also a time to celebrate the success of the work you did throughout the spring and summer. Winter is a time for rest, reflection, and planning for the future. These simple lessons from nature can help you gain an understanding of the seasons in your life.

Quality of Life

Many people get stuck in the rut of making a living for their entire lives. Making a living is a season of life, it is not all of life. People get stuck by focusing only on finances and neglecting the other areas of their life. Making a living is just one of the F's: faith, family, friends, fitness, and finances. Each area is important and they all influence each other.

Look at your hand. Let your index finger represent your faith, your middle finger is your family, your ring finger is your friends, your pinky is your fitness, and your thumb is your finances. Notice how easily your thumb can touch each of your other fingers. So, it is with your finances. Increasing your income and learning to build wealth can enable you to give more to the charities and causes you believe in. It allows you to spend more time with your family and friends; it gives you more time to exercise and do hobbies that help you stay strong and healthy.

It is a worthy goal to increase your standard of living.

Thus, it is a worthy goal to increase your standard of living, just make sure that you are also focused on increasing your quality of life at the same time. If you only focus on raising your standard of living, then chances are that you will lower your quality of life. When you balance each area of life, then you can raise your quality of life and standard of living at the same time.

Building anything takes time, especially building a life. When you learn to be patient with the process of life, you will enjoy it more. It takes a lifetime to build a life. Dreams don't have deadlines.

Dream fulfillers build a life.

Dream killers make a living.

DISTINCTION SIX

Dream fulfillers are awake.

Dream killers are asleep.

Overeating and overdrinking put you to sleep, especially if you eat unnatural and processed foods or drink toxic liquids. This relates to your physical as well as your spiritual, emotional, and mental lives.

To keep it simple, let's consider your physical life your outer life, and your spiritual, emotional, and mental lives your inner life. Of course, your inner life is directly linked to your outer life and whatever you do to your inner life affects your outer life, and vice versa.

For example, if you overeat food that is full of chemicals and other ingredients your body can't digest and utilize, you will feel down and experience low energy, both emotionally and mentally. But, if you eat food that is natural and unprocessed, like fresh fruits and vegetables,

> Whatever you do to your inner life affects your outer life, and vice versa.

then you will feel alive. You will notice that you are happier emotionally and mentally and able to think more clearly.

Physically you eat with your mouth; spiritually, emotionally, and mentally you eat with your eyes and ears. What are you putting into your eyes and ears? What do you watch and listen to on a consistent basis? If you ingest too much death and negativity into your inner life you will fall asleep spiritually, emotionally, and mentally. People who are asleep in their inner lives are stuck in a routine of mediocrity; they just go through the motions of living but are not awake. Overeating things that are not healthy or positive put you into a deep sleep. Dream killers are like zombies.

The way dream fulfillers stay awake is by feeding their inner lives with messages that are alive and positive. Watch and listen to things that encourage and inspire you and you will stay awake. Hope is alive; love is alive. Feed your faith with hope and love and you remain awake. When you are awake you are aware. Being awake and aware means you can discern between what is healthy and unhealthy for your inner life.

Sometimes people know something is bad for them and they ingest it anyway. Usually this is because what is bad for you oftentimes tastes or feels good. For example, my dad gets a headache almost every time he eats chocolate but he still eats chocolate. In fact, while he is eating it he'll say, "I'm going to regret this later."

Have you ever done something that felt good at the moment but you knew you were going to regret later?

Consider Thanksgiving dinner. After most people overeat they say, "Why did I do that?"

Then they take a nap. I've done that same thing in my inner life with TV and movies. I used to sit and flip through the channels for an hour and then wake up and realize I just wasted an hour. Or I'd find a show that hooked me and I'd watch it and sit through all the commercials and after an hour or two I'd realize I just fed my heart and mind a bunch of junk. For years now we have not had cable TV in our home because so much of what comes across TV is dead.

> Dream fulfillers invest their money on things that encourage and inspire them to keep taking action.

Most people continually feed their inner life things that are dead, like the extremely bad news that comes through most of the media. Dream fulfillers invest their money on things that encourage and inspire them to keep taking action. Remember, what you eat and drink through your eyes and ears will affect the way you feel physically and what you eat and drink physically will affect your inner life. So, eat some good books that encourage you and drink some good movies that will inspire you. Be careful what you put into your eyes and ears. Stay awake and take consistent action towards your dream.

Dream fulfillers are awake.

Dream killers are asleep.

DISTINCTION FIVE

Dream fulfillers are happy and healthy.

Dream killers are depressed and sick.

Most people understand that being happy helps people be healthier. It was written thousands of years ago in Scripture that "A cheerful heart does good like a medicine." There are also modern-day stories of people who had terrible illnesses and who healed themselves through laughter.

Being happy improves your health. One of the Scriptures that I meditate on regularly is "The joy of the Lord is our strength." Think about how you feel when you are happy versus when you are depressed. Happiness creates health and strength; depression creates sickness and weakness. If you want to be healthier and stronger then learn to be happy.

> If you want to be healthier and stronger then learn to be happy.

Happiness and depression are simply results of the choices you make. Yes, people choose to be either happy or depressed. Many people have been trained or conditioned to be angry, negative, and depressed, so it may not seem like they have a choice—but they do.

In my life, happiness and depression are the results of what I choose to focus on. What you focus on, you feel. Focus on your disappointments and things you don't like and you will feel bad and that will play out in your physical health. Focus on the good in your life and in this world and you will feel happy, which will also play out in your health.

> Focus on the good in your life and in this world and you will feel happy,

You can prove this to yourself right now by simply thinking about something you enjoy or someone you love and notice how you feel in your body. Then, think about something you don't like or someone who has hurt you and then notice how you feel in your body. It is a wonderful day when you realize you can improve your health by your thoughts and it is an incredible moment every time you choose to shift your focus from something negative to something positive.

Happiness and depression are the result of what you choose to focus on. For the people who have been conditioned to be negative from the time when they were very young it is a challenge and even downright difficult to choose to be happy. They have habitual thought patterns that keep them unhappy which leads to depression and sickness.

> Happiness and depression are the result of what you choose to focus on.

Scripture says, "Be transformed by the renewing of your mind." To move from depression to happiness is transformation. You make the move by choosing to think about or focus on things that produce peace and joy. For most people it takes a conscious effort to focus on the good. There are people who are blessed by having been trained or conditioned to be optimistic, and happiness comes easier for them. If you have been conditioned to be negative, you can take responsibility for your thoughts and be transformed. It is up to you to renew your mind.

Focus on the good and positive aspects of life. Practice looking for what is funny in your life. Remember, seek and you will find. If you look for what is funny you will find it, and then laugh about it. Laughter truly is good medicine for your body and your mind.

Inner and Outer Exercise

Whatever you can do to be happier, do it; it will improve your health. Whatever you can do to be healthier, do it; it will improve your happiness.

Have you ever noticed that when you are physically active you feel better emotionally? Your physical body and your Spirit and soul are intricately connected and they affect each other. Everyone knows that physical exercise improves mental health. It is easier to be happy when you are regularly engaged in physical exercise.

It is important to feed your faith.

Inner exercise causes your heart, mind, and body to feel strong and happy. Inner exercise is simply to believe in your dream; it is to practice believing the best about yourself and others. Inner exercise is to exercise your faith. It is important to feed your faith and to exercise it. If you overeat physically without exercising you can become overweight or even obese. People do this mentally and emotionally by going to one seminar after another and continually reading self-help books and then never applying what they learn. If you have become fat in your inner life, you can lose weight there the same way you can in your outer life—by changing what you eat and drink and adding regular exercise. This is true of your physical body just as it is for your Spirit and soul.

By focusing on your dream you feed your heart and mind; by choosing to believe in your dream, you are exercising your heart and mind. So, feed your inner life by focusing on your dream and exercise your inner life by believing it is possible and then see if you don't experience more happiness and health.

Have hope in your dream. Hope feeds faith. There is a Proverb that says "Hope deferred makes the heart sick." Hope is related to happiness. You can't experience happiness and hope-lessness at the same time. If you don't choose to have hope for your dream, you may find your-self battling with depression and sickness. Have hope, believe in your dream, and choose to be happy and healthy.

Dream fulfillers are happy and healthy.

Dream killers are depressed and sick.

DISTINCTION FOUR

Dream fulfillers believe in principles.

Dream killers believe in
situational ethics.

Principles are eternal, they do not change. Principles stand the test of time. They were true yesterday, are true today, and will be true tomorrow. Living your life by principles is like building your house on rock. Living by situational ethics is like building your house on sand, i.e., situational ethics shift and change with the tides. Living by situational ethics means you alter your beliefs depending on what is popular at the moment. A life governed by situational ethics is one lived in confusion and frustration. With situational ethics you don't have a belief or faith that you can depend on because they are subject to change with the shifting sands of the masses.

> People who live by principles are solid and strong.

People who live by principles are solid and strong; they enjoy a security and peace that the masses do not understand. They do not change their beliefs simply because something becomes unpopular. They are people of conscience. They listen to the still, small voice within their hearts. They are not perfect, rather they are being perfected and becoming more, doing more, and having more.

Principles are the path to purpose, peace, and prosperity. Principles create peace in your heart and mind. They empower you to fulfill your purpose. Without principles, life is shallow and void of meaning.

> Principles are the path to purpose, peace, and prosperity.

People who live by situational ethics do not know what their purpose in life is and they usually experience constant stress and poverty. Not just financial poverty but poverty of spirit. The poorest person on the planet is one who does not know his or her purpose for living. People of principle have a deep understanding that their primary purpose in life is to live by principles. I realize that might not sound deep or enlightening but the understanding that principles lead to a life of purpose, peace, and prosperity is the understanding that living by principles is your purpose.

What are some of these principles that lead to prosperity? It is beyond the scope of this one distinction to discuss most of them but I will mention the most important principle that encompasses many others. The book of Proverbs in the Old Testament is full of principles; I strongly suggest reading from it often, even daily. The most important principle is love. Love is patient, kind, and forgiving. Dream fulfillers BELIEVE in principles. Do you believe in love? Do you believe in patience, kindness, and forgiveness? If you do, then you practice them. It doesn't mean you are perfect, it means you practice. Love, patience, kindness, and for-giveness are the path to purpose, peace, and prosperity.

Dream killers do not practice love. They practice selfishness. They are always changing their beliefs based on what's in it for them. If they believe they can get more for themselves by changing their beliefs, they do so. Situational ethics are about self; prin-ciples are about people. Situational ethics put profits above people. Principles put people above profits. Love is not selfish, it is generous. Patience, kindness, and forgiveness are directly the opposite of situational ethics and selfishness.

Principles put people above profits.

Dream fulfillers believe in principles.

Dream killers believe in situational ethics.

DISTINCTION THREE

Dream fulfillers walk through
the valley.

Dream killers pitch a tent in
the valley.

"Multitudes, multitudes in the valley of decision!" Lack of decision is the valley of death. Stay there and you will kill your dream. To fulfill your dream you must consistently make wise decisions. Sometimes you make wise decisions and sometimes you will make foolish decisions—which give you valuable information to learn from. Everyone makes mistakes, even dream fulfillers.

Dream killers are afraid to make mistakes so they just pitch a tent in the valley. Ask dream killers what they are going to do about their dream and they will respond, "I don't know what to do, so I am not going to do anything." Many times what they really mean is that they are afraid to make a mistake so they are not going to do anything. Fear and lack of decision-making leads to unfulfilled dreams.

Do you know what your dream is? If so,

make decisions that move you toward it and don't worry about making mistakes because they are a valuable part of the process. Making decisions that keep you moving toward your dream is wisdom even if some of them turn out to be mistakes. Everyone stumbles and falls sometimes but as long as you are taking steps in the direction of your dream then you are getting closer to seeing it fulfilled even with the mistakes you make. The biggest mistake you could ever make is to sit in the valley and do nothing.

Everyone stumbles and falls sometimes.

Make Decisions Based in Faith

It is wisdom to make decisions based in faith. When you take action because of fear it is usually the wrong action, even if it is non-action. Fear hinders the flow of wisdom that is within your heart. Faith unlocks the divine wisdom that is required to fulfill your dream. When you are confronted with a decision, make it in faith; believe that things will go well—sometimes they will and sometimes they won't. When you make a decision based in faith and the result appears to be negative, look for a lesson that the mistake is bringing you. As long as you learn from your mistakes, then they are actually successes.

If you make decisions based in fear they will most likely go wrong. In other words, you usually get the exact opposite of what you want, which is the very thing you were afraid of. Fear is a terrible enemy of dreams; faith is a wonderful friend to dreams.

Faith is closely related to wisdom; wisdom is the ability to make the right decisions. One of the primary decisions that you will have to make many, many times before seeing your dream fulfilled is the decision to keep going. It is always a wise decision to keep going. When you choose to persevere it proves you are making a decision based in faith because you would not choose to keep going unless you believed that you can fulfill your dream.

> As long as you learn from your mistakes, then they are actually successes.

The reason it is wisdom to keep going when you are in a valley is because valleys are connected to peaks. As long as you keep going, you will eventually find yourself on top of a mountain. And remember, when you get to the top of a mountain, there is a valley on the other side. Everyone goes through many peaks and valleys in pursuit of their dreams.

No matter what your life situation is today it will change soon if you keep going after your dream. The life of a dream fulfiller is constantly changing. Sometimes for the better and sometimes for what seems like the worse. But, through it all, you will constantly be confronted with decisions. Learn to make decisions based in faith and you will experience more peaks and valleys. You will learn more and accomplish more. Make decisions based in fear and you will remain basically the same.

So, make the decision to go for it! Take consistent action toward your dream, especially when you find yourself in a valley, because you want to see the view from the top of the next peak. Pitching a tent in the valley means you have stopped moving toward your dream. Make the decision to keep going.

Dream fulfillers walk through the valley.

Dream killers pitch a tent in the valley.

DISTINCTION TWO

Dream fulfillers believe in destiny.

Dream killers believe in chance and coincidence.

Do you believe in destiny? If you do, then that means there is something you are supposed to be doing with your life. Your destiny is your dream. And, although it is "your" dream, you can't fulfill it without others, which means there are people you are supposed to be in relationship with.

There are people you are destined to be in relationship with and there are people you are destined not to be in relationship with. Many times when God wants to bless you, He will send a person. And when the enemy wants to curse you, he will send a person. Therefore, it is extremely important that you are in relationships that you are supposed to be in and that you stay away from people who you are not supposed to be in relationship with so that you can do what you are supposed to be doing with your life.

Sometimes when you first meet people it will require patience to determine if they are someone whom you are supposed to be in relationship with. Be careful with first impressions. First impressions are lasting impressions but they are not necessarily accurate perceptions. The way you see a person is the way you judge a person and judgments are based on your own prejudices. A prejudice is simply a pre-judgment. It is unwise to pre-judge

> First impressions are lasting impressions but they are not necessarily accurate perceptions.

people. It takes time to get to really know someone. After awhile you will be able to see clearly if someone is supposed to be a part of your destiny, your dream.

In my experience, there are four types of people: people who are supposed to help you, people you are supposed to help, people who you help and they help you in return, and people who you are supposed to avoid like the plague. Most people you meet can either help you or you can help them; a few people you need to run from. The key is identifying which category people fall in. You may think someone is supposed to help you but in reality your destiny is to help them. Or you may think you are supposed to help someone but their destiny is to help you. This is where God's sense of humor shows up. Initially, you might even think you need to run from someone but that person might have some knowledge or be a contact that is important to your dream.

> Be very careful about prejudging people as you could lose a key piece of the puzzle to your dream.

Millions of dreams have been delayed because people's prejudices make them judge someone as unworthy of their time and energy, so they avoid them—when, in actuality, they are a vital part of their destiny. Be very careful about pre-judging people as you could lose a key piece of the puzzle to your dream.

Warning: get away and stay away from people who you know for certain you are not supposed to be in relationship with. If you have known someone for awhile and you know that there is no opportunity for you to help them or there is no opportunity for them to help you, then move on. (I am not talking about marriage. There are only a few specific reasons to move on from a spouse, like abuse and sexual immorality, but that's another book.) I am talking about friends, colleagues, and people you see on a regular basis. If there is someone who is constantly feeding your fear and draining you, then you must move away or suffer the consequences. The consequences are a delayed dream, which can become a dead dream and an unfulfilled life.

Make no mistake, the people in your life are not there by accident, chance, or coincidence. Some people come into your life for definite purposes that either help or hinder your destiny. Some people are either supposed to bless your dream or be blessed by you. And, a small minority come into your life with the purpose to destroy your dream. Dream fulfillers do what they can to help others fulfill their dreams and dream killers, who have already killed their own dreams, do what they can to kill the dreams of others.

> Dream fulfillers do what they can to help others fulfill their dreams.

Contrary to common thinking, your destiny or dream is not set in stone. It is flexible and dynamic. It can expand and grow or it can get smaller and die depending on YOU and the people you are in relationship with. The people that you choose to associate with are either supposed to be in your life or not. Choose to build relationships with those who are and you will fulfill your destiny.

Dream fulfillers believe in destiny.

Dream killers believe in chance and coincidence.

DISTINCTION ONE

**Dream fulfillers know the
Dream Giver.**

Dream killers know the destroyer.

God is the Dream Giver. The Dream Giver said, "I have come that you may have life and have it more abundantly." Right before He said that, He said this about the destroyer: "The thief comes to kill, steal and destroy." The Dream Giver also called the destroyer the father of lies. How does the destroyer destroy your dream and eventually your life? Through lies. Lies about God, lies about yourself, and lies about other people.

If you don't believe in God, then ask yourself "If there is no God, why do I have a dream inside of me? Where did it come from?" The only answer is that God put it there. If there is no God then nothing has any meaning and everyone would be living like animals. You may say, "Well, a lot of people *do* live like animals." That is true, but there are those who seek to live by faith versus being victims of fear. People who do not know the Dream Giver will always live in fear and continually experience stress, doubt, and worry. Those who know the Dream Giver will learn to overcome fear and live by faith, which produces peace and joy.

> There are those who seek to live by faith versus being victims of fear.

Pursuing your dream will require you to face your fears and achieving your dream will require you to overcome them. Where does fear come from? It comes from believing lies. One of the biggest lies is that there is no God.

Three Big Lies and Three Great Truths

The three big lies are:

- There is no God.

- He doesn't love you.

- You can't fulfill your dream.

The three great truths are:

- There is a God.

- He does love you.

- You can fulfill your dream.

Imagine the following conversation:

Destroyer: "There is no God."

You: "Yes, there is."

Destroyer: "Okay there is a God but He doesn't love you. I mean, how could He? You are so screwed up and you fail all the time."

You: "Yes, there is a God and He loves me unconditionally."

Destroyer: "Okay, there is a God and He loves you, but you can't fulfill your dream. It's impossible."

You: "With God, all things are possible; so yes, I can fulfill my dream."

Have you ever had a conversation in your heart or mind that is similar to this? To believe the destroyer, means you agree with his lies. To be free of him all you must do is believe the truth. There is a God, He loves you, and you can fulfill your dream.

Your success is dependent on who you are connected to. You listen to people you are connected to. Listen to the truth of the Dream Giver and you can and will fulfill your dream. Listen to the lies of the destroyer and your life will be filled with fear, doubt, worry, and stress.

> Your success is dependent on who you are connected to.

Here is a clue on how to discern between the Dream Giver's voice and the destroyer's. The Dream Giver's voice speaks through your heart and the destroyer's voice speaks to your mind. Your heart is full of faith, hope, and love. Your mind is based in fear, doubt, and anger. Your heart and mind have conflicting desires. To become a dream fulfiller you must learn to discern between the deep desires of your heart and the deceptive desires of your mind.

The deep desires of your heart are put there by the Dream Giver. Consider the words *desire* and *inspire*. The root meaning of the word *desire* is "of the Father." The root meaning of the word *inspire* is "in the Spirit." The desires that inspire you were put in your heart by the Dream Giver. Learn to listen to and follow your heart.

> Deceptive desires are first and foremost based on lies.

The deceptive desires that the destroyer puts into your mind are things that you think will make you happy and fulfilled but they can't. Deceptive desires are first and foremost based on lies. The deep desires of your heart are based on truth. Truth creates peace; lies create stress. When your head and heart are arguing you will experience confusion. To get rid of confusion listen to your heart and tell your head, your fears, to shut up and then do what the Dream Giver is telling you to do through your heart.

Your heart knows the way. Your mind is confused. Your heart is peaceful. Your mind is stressed. The reason your heart is full of faith, hope, love, and peace and knows the way is because that is where the Dream Giver resides. Don't you know that you are the temple of the Holy Spirit? The Holy Spirit is the Dream Giver and lives within you. I am not talking about religion I am talking about truth. Truth transcends religion. (If you are interested in my views and experiences with religion, please read my book *The Top 10 Distinctions between Relationship and Religion*.)

Inspiration and encouragement are a benefit of being in relationship with the Dream Giver. It takes continual inspiration and encouragement to keep moving toward your dream. One of the primary reasons people don't take action on their dreams is because they are waiting for someone else to give them permission to do so. Here is the truth: You don't need anyone's permission to pursue your dreams because you already have the permission of the One who gave you the dream. Get to know Him. One of the prayers in Scriptures is "That I may know Him and the power of His resurrection."

Perhaps the destroyer has killed your dream. Well, here's another truth: God can resurrect your dream. To become a dream fulfiller you may have to go through the death and resurrection of your dream.

Maybe your dream isn't dead, maybe it is

simply asleep and all you need to do is ask the Dream Giver to help you wake it up. If you do, then be ready for a shaking. If you have fallen asleep because of eating too many lies, maybe God is shaking you to wake you up. He is waking you up because you have a

> To become a dream fulfiller you may have to go through the death and resurrection of your dream.

dream to fulfill. Wake up, get up, stay up. Persevere until you fulfill your dream and in the end the Dream Giver will give you a crown of life. If you know the Dream Giver, then always remember this: in the end, everything will be fine. If everything is not fine, then it is not the end.

Dream fulfillers know the Dream Giver.

Dream killers know the destroyer.

What Now?

Read this book often. I recommend reading it once a month until you feel the ten distinctions have become a part of who you are. Repetition is the primary way we train our minds to think differently. When we think differently, we act differently and achieve different results.

Share copies of this book with the important people in your life so you can discuss the distinctions and learn from one another's experiences and perspectives.

Go to www.keithcameronsmith.com and

register for the Wise Distinctions email to receive continued support in developing your mind-set for a positive attitude and success.

You can also join me for teleseminars and get information about upcoming Wisdom Creates Freedom workshops.

About the Author

KEITH CAMERON SMITH is an entrepreneur and inspirational speaker who teaches his life-success principles to individuals and companies around the country. The author of *The Spiritual Millionaire*, *The Top 10 Distinctions between Millionaires and the Middle Class*, and other books, Smith lives in Ormond Beach, Florida, with his wife and their two children.

Visit his website: keithcameronsmith.com

Other books by Keith Cameron Smith

THE TOP 10 DISTINCTIONS BETWEEN
MILLIONAIRES AND THE MIDDLE CLASS

THE TOP 10 DISTINCTIONS BETWEEN
ENTREPRENEURS AND EMPLOYEES

THE TOP 10 DISTINCTIONS BETWEEN
RELATIONSHIP AND RELIGION

THE TOP 10 DISTINCTIONS BETWEEN
WINNERS AND WHINERS

100 DISTINCTIONS BETWEEN
SUCCESS AND FAILURE

THE SPIRITUAL MILLIONAIRE: THE SPIRIT
OF WISDOM WILL MAKE YOU RICH

For more information, please visit:

www.keithcameronsmith.com